Shame Shame Shame

A Poetic Chapbook

Miss Imani.
Illustrations by:
Pamela Walsh Arts

Copyright © 2025 Miss Imani, Pamela Walsh Arts, Malcolm Scott
All rights reserved.
The Amazon Endure typeface was designed by 2K/DENMARK in 2025.
Template id: ST-414D415A-25-A01
Printed in The United States.
ISBN: 9798993513607

DEDICATION

To everyone I have ever loved...
And anyone I have ever hurt.
I hope you'll take this book
As a token to be preserved.

Special thanks to Josh, Pam, Nikita, Rayne
and every single soul in the
community we've created online.
I literally couldn't have
done this without y'all.

And thank you to the amazing authors
who gave me their time and energy
to help make sure my first book was
beautiful. Tia, Roderick, and Licia:
Y'all are truly the best!

CONTENTS

	Author's Note	i
1	Imani's Got Pockets	1
2	On Display	2
3	Abandoned	3
4	To My Past Lovers	4
5	Untitled	5
6	You're Happy	6
7	We Danced	8
8	Until I See Your Name	9
9	Disgusted	11
10	I Could Have Said It	12
11	Marked	13
12	Why Would You	14
13	Speak Child, Speak!	16
14	Speak Child, Speak Take Two	17
15	*A Dedication*	19
16	Mama	20
17	If I Could Save Her	22
18	Over and Over Again	23
19	Letter to Hurricane Milton	24
20	Father	25
21	Mistake	26
22	To Be a Girl	27
23	My Fault Too	29
24	Crush	30
25	*A Dedication*	32
26	Arms	33
27	Acacia	34
28	I Did You a Favor	35
29	Pro-Choice	36
30	How Do I Tell Them	37
31	Your Daddy	38
32	I Tried	40
33	Let Go	41
34	The Color of My Skin	42
35	The Other Side of Pain	43
36	Passing It Down	44
37	Yume Was Here	45
38	6 of Swords	46
39	Lay it Down	47

SHAME, SHAME, SHAME

AUTHOR'S NOTE

As you read through this book, you may ask yourself: "Why is she ashamed of this?" I have a mixture of lighthearted to downright dark poems and letters included in this work, and it may confuse some as to why the "good" ones would be considered shameful. Well, dear reader, to put it simply—I couldn't talk about it. I've been through many trials throughout my life, many of which were self-inflicted, and more often than not—I was mocked, ridiculed, ostracized, or even forced into isolation by those I held dearest to me. My words tend to be sharp and cutting, often cutting too deeply. I tend to leave my patients open, bleeding, and exposed on the table after seeing deeper than I should, and I was not equipped with the tools necessary to close the wound. So here I am, practicing on myself. Cutting deep and exposing my organs for all to see, so that one day...I'll stop leaving the ones I love on the table to die.

Trigger warning: This work contains material not suitable for minors. The content of this work touches on sensitive topics, such as multiple types of abuse. Please read with caution and contact a trusted professional if necessary.

"Behavior is the mirror in which everyone shows their image."
~
Johann Wolfgang Von Goethe

1 IMANI'S GOT POCKETS

Hi.
My name is Imani and I've got a lot to share.
In my pockets I hold both my hopes and my fears,
as well as my faults and my talents.
My trauma and my achievements are stored there too,
Stories never told, tales you couldn't believe are true.
Imani's got a lot of problems and not enough solutions.
You'd think the bags she carried would encourage her to let loose
and be the woman god intended her to be.
Imani struggles with feeling like she's even a little bit free.
Imani's got a lot of acquaintances.
You can't say friends now because friends can't be *enemies*
But *acquaintances* can be *anything*.
I mean, Imani's got a lot of people who could be listening,
So she should be careful of what she says.
Imani's pockets have been used against her so much she often wishes
She were dead.
Imani can't make decisions without talking to someone
About it first but, Imani hates confrontation.
Bitter words are akin to a hearse.
But in Imani's pockets she holds something special,
and everyone wants to know what it is.
Well, I'm here to let you know that
the only thing there is to know
is that—
Imani is still
UNFINISHED.

2 ON DISPLAY

My biggest fear has always been
Being forgotten, and to be remembered:
People would have to know me.
I would have to come out of my shell
And let the world know that *I* am here.
Though that's another thing I fear.
I've walked this earth with my eyes covered,
Ears opened and lips shut.
Ripping and shredding time, relationships
and myself apart so that I could, subconsciously,
leave some kind of mark on this world.
All of my sins would come to light.
I know because there are those who would love to see
Me fall out of spite.
What of my family should I follow glory?
What of my name after it's been sullied?
I fear so much of what my past may say,
Unless I should just hide away and pray?
Repetition of self-sabotage is what
That is, I've hidden in fear for years.
Nothing, no one else.
Has stopped me from success.
Yet, I craft and crave
A life on a stage where the lights are too bright
To see any one face.
I just want to create and use my voice.
I want to dance and fake all the emotions in the world.
Recite lines and give back to the people I left behind…
Because I haven't forgotten. I've just been hiding.
I have grown and now I know
That the marks I made were scars, damage that will never go away.
If I chased glory now…All my sins would be on display.

3 ABANDONED

I'm so afraid of being abandoned
That you're not allowed to get too close
And if you get close enough to my heart
I'll never let you go.
The people-pleaser in me will do the absolute most,
Lick your tender bits with a softness after I dig
Into your wounds with my words.
I've already laid my wrists bare for you to stare.
The wounds left there are begging to be explored,
Silently asking you for more.
I just want to be accepted by you,
Wanted—no—needed by you.
I need to have a reason to
Run from you
Or I won't have a reason to stay by you.
And if this season is not meant to be with you
Then I won't speak to you again.
It's better if I leave first, better for you in the end.
My rage is dangerous, toxic and intense.
If you abandon me, then we will both meet our deaths.

4 TO MY PAST LOVERS

As I grow older
I become more aware
Of how I acted in love,
Doing things that wasn't fair.
I blamed and accused despite
My many messy moods and
When it came down to
Displaying my own dirty truth
I choose to turn away
And pretend I am obtuse.
Only now I know
I was not pretending,
I was not fully aware.
The way that I acted in love
Was because I was not really
There.
I'm in my head
More often than not
And when you care for
Another
It's not just
You anymore
And that's something I never
got.
I thought being the good girl
Would get me what I want
But never spoke up
When my boundaries were
Crossed.
Instead I maneuvered,
Manipulated and cheated
Back then my middle name
Should have been
"Deceiver"
So here's my public
statement of accountability
I am sorry I blamed
It all on you
When I never even
gave you
all of me.

5 UNTITLED

I am strong.
Powerful.
A frightening force of nature.
An omen.
Your karma.
Proof that your god exists.
Patient and kind, generous and humble
But the moment that love comes into play
my entire existence begins to crumble.
My brain cannot keep up with the daily routine of my life.
The only thing it wants to focus on is
Your voice and what our future may be
like?
And though there are more pressing matters to attend to
my mind will continuously circle back to
you.
Except this time I wonder if you'll treat
me good?
I wonder if I'll be made a fool.
I wonder then more and more until its less wonder and more anxiety I harbor—
Am I even good enough?

Who would want me?

You remember what happened last time
right?
You'll be left alone again soon, you'll see.
And to block it all out I give into the
pressure.
You can't drown me if I'm above water. I prepare my lifeboat with a badge of honor.
I'll criticize and pick and make an
accusation fit
as long as in my mind I'm safe again
THAT'S IT!
I've pushed you away
and now the voices have left me to play
with my self-loathing and self-pity
because I'll always be alone.
But at least I'll be strong.
At least I can handle better the days that
come along.
And if I have to sacrifice love to stay alive
then I think it's a worth sacrifice
because my life is not mine alone.
And I'll be damned if I give up again
just because you didn't answer your
phone.

6 YOU'RE HAPPY

My chest feels tight with fear.
Your absence is like the headlights
and I'm a frozen deer.
Have I lost you for good this time?
Did I push our relationship past the point of no repair?
Please call me—Message me back.
I promise I'm not looking to attack
this time.
I seem to have woken from a dream
Where I was the victim and you were both
The key and my need.
My addiction, that you would so graciously feed.
But *this time* you say you're happy,
That we've already said goodbye—
Maybe I don't understand?
It's not like we hadn't said that like 10 other times?
This time
You don't respond.
You grew tired of the off and on
Hey!
I'm tired too and like I said I have woken up to the truth—
There was no victim.
We both hurt each other.
I took the good and the bad
And mixed them up with each other.
I blamed you when I went down the wrong path
When I could have kept
The one thing of me you asked.
So this time you have yet to come back,
And now I can't breathe.
There are so many things I've come to
Regret now that I'm awake.
I burn myself recalling
Every. Little. Mistake.
Reading between lines from conversations years past,
That I just didn't catch at the time.
How you always knew the deepest thoughts in my mind.
I didn't HAVE to speak.
You knew all my words and somehow,
deep down, you even knew
How much I was worth.
Underneath the trauma mask I wore,
You saw me for something Amazing.
Something much, much more.
And with all the words I have yet to say,
I wish I could tell you how much you meant to me.
So much so that you became
My air.
Now I'm paying to find relief.
I wish I knew how high

SHAME, SHAME, SHAME

The price would be.
I wish I had listened when
You tried to talk to me.
I wish I had been mature enough
To understand,
What you meant when you said that
I had never loved a man.

7 WE DANCED

I always said I would never be
"That Girl"
I am wholesome and of good intent.
However when I met him,
I swore that he was heaven sent.
So, we danced.
We danced under the moonlight,
hidden from the spotlight.
Slowly in the dark.
Hip to hip.
Heart to heart.
We loved every minute of that night.
You wouldn't know because he told me
You were "just not right."
You know what he told me?
He said:
"I only got her pregnant because she's pretty. "
And we danced.
Though I never noticed how *silly*
I looked with a man who
Never honored the woman
Who he made a child with.
But we danced,
And I stared into his eyes.
I let his gaze hypnotize me.
I let him fill my head with lies.
And even though the same was done to me,
I passed the hurt on and now I'm ashamed of me.
But, we danced.

8 UNTIL I SEE YOUR NAME

It's crazy how I never noticed
how many people shared the same name as you before we met.
I hate the way my body seizes
and my heart pounds till it pops
the stitches I placed when I see
the "C" at the start of a name.
My greatest love and deepest betrayal,
Time for me had stopped and new attempts at love have failed
and I cry because I will probably never
know love again.
You're not forgiven.
For three times I gave too much of I
and let you spread my skin on the bed
for you to roll around in with your new bitch like sheets.
I write about you still because I am angry.
Because I am disappointed.
And when I see your name it floods back
like a wound that never closes.
How could I ever love another man
when my body aches like this?
It's as if I'm sick with disease
And only your smile,
your laugh,
the twinkle in your eyes and the frown
when you're mad,
only you could ease this sickness
but you're the facilitator of this illness.
You're the reason I second-guess my judgment
and retrace my steps.
Why I pinch the skin around my waist
and frown in the mirror when I pass.
Because standing there staring
would take all day comparing
my body to theirs.

I'm so quick to leave
because no one's allowed to hurt me like
you did.
I hesitate when they want to get deep
because they might use it against me like
you did.
I shatter in silence and am rebuilt by attention
but I question my self-worth daily

SHAME, SHAME, SHAME

because you didn't claim me.
So I hide my hope and never fall for
maybe's.
And I'm okay,

until I see your name.

9 DISGUSTED

I'm so disgusted with myself
For the things I was taught too young.
The misguided acts I did in hopes of receiving love.
The journey to self-love is muddy with shame and
Regret, my feet get stuck every few steps I take.
Still the disgust I cannot shake.
How could I have enjoyed what was done to me?
How could I have coveted what didn't belong to me?
How could I have stooped to levels so low that my moral compass looks
Broken to those I do not know?
I thought doing what felt good was doing what was right,
I thought doing what I was taught would bring me closer to life
But I was misled and used and made to believe that the abuse was all I would amount to.
One day I hope that this feeling goes away,
I'd love to be happy in love without feeling insecure about my worth or what I say.

10 I COULD HAVE SAID IT

You know, I really could have said it.
The very sentence that would put you in a grave.
My tongue is sharp like a Japanese blade,
You wouldn't even have the chance to utter the words
"Wait, My mistake."
You'll bleed out all over me and call me a demon
When, you just let go of the knife in my back.
Like I didn't just suffer at your hands from a sideways attack.
Life you didn't just try to diminish my light because you're insecure that I'll
Illuminate your darkness and laugh in delight
Like I'm not here for love and to find creative fires to ignite.
I inspire you—
But you can't spare me a kind word?
Is my inspiration only enough to bring back YOUR self-worth?
If I had known I was going to be treated like filth at the hands of another,
I could have said what I wanted.
I really could have said it.

SHAME, SHAME, SHAME

11 MARKED

Out of all the times that I've been hit
You're the first to leave a mark.
On my mind, on my face, and on my soul too.
I will never be the same, and that's all thanks to you.
In my heart, I know I played a part.
But you took it too far,
And you knew you would from the start.
The last time it was foot, to face, to concrete.
I still remember the dizziness and my struggling to breathe.
This time you put your knees on my arms to stop me,
Sat on my waist so I couldn't move.
I guess my hands are a little heavy for a
Silly Puss in boots.
Never have I known fear like this,
I long for the day that I will forget—
Because the scream I choked out
At the top of the stairs,
Shook me to my core and
Still echoes in my ears.
I hope you meet your match someday,
I know revenge is cruel.
But I hope they blacken your face the same way
So maybe...that maybe it matches your soul.

12 WHY WOULD YOU

Why would you love me,
When my skin has been touched
By hands too rough.
Made impure by
The fingers of men with more
Experience than I.
Why would you love me,
When this skin you praise has been,
Desecrated by white fluids.
Secreted from perversion.
Why would you love me,
When this body was defiled
Before I was even old
Enough to understand sin?
Why would you love me,
When the personality I present
Is an indicator of where I've been?

"In every conceivable manner, the family is [li]nk to our past, bridge to our future."

~ Alex Haley

SHAME, SHAME, SHAME

13 SPEAK CHILD, SPEAK!

Speak child speak,
Hold not your tongue...
Because the Questions that
you may ask
the answers that it brings
may be the solution that
saves us all.
Speak child speak,
Because ignorance is not
bliss
it is apathy to the mind,
it is the residue of
brainwashed thoughts
that destroys itself fully with
passions of
time,
Stagnation is ignorance and
the death of
young and old minds.
Speak child speak
Your voice may be the one
that touches the world and
reshapes
reality
into a peaceable paradise
that woman,
men, and children may grow
and live in.

Speak child speak
Because my voice is old and
unremembered
it is the weeping of slaves in
the bowels
of coffin ships
it is the creak of rope and
wood
and silent kingdoms swaying
in a sultry
southern breeze,
it is the shackles of
falsehood binding me to
inferior thoughts
of medieval slavery,
it is the sound of a fast life
lived and lost in court rooms
trying to escape my self-
created hell.
Speak child speak,
Because you are the grace
of god
and the dreams of a nation.

Speak Child Speak!

~ Malcolm Scott (my father)

14 SPEAK CHILD, SPEAK TAKE TWO

Speak child, speak
He says. And when I turn to open my lips
A hand comes and forces me to "stand down"
Speak child speak,
My mind is racing with thoughts,
Spinning and swirling while
my face barely wears a frown.

I was not allowed to show how I felt.
I was not allowed to be a little girl.
I was not allowed to speak my thoughts,
Or believe my words could change the world.

It's hard to believe that anyone
Wants to hear me
That my words have weight
Speak child, speak
He says
Even if you make a mistake.

If his voice is old and unremembered
Then what is mine?
I feel young and naive but
My age has doubled since
The last time I read what he writes.
My voice holds pain too.
Pain even then too much to
Thrive through—
in
my voice you hear
Little girls being neglected and used.
Mothers doing drugs just to get over her blues.
Grandmothers who won't leave because to her
With a man is safer than being free.
I can't speak for us all.
Yet I've bled for us all,

SHAME, SHAME, SHAME

And no one has opened their mouth.
I was just a child,
My voice was too small to be heard,
But I'm older now and I'm speaking up.
I'm not a child now but the children need us.
Speak child speak was not a message for me.
Speak. Child. Speak.
So we can all be free!

15 *A DEDICATION*

Mom,

I know that this book will hurt you. It is not my intention to do so, no matter how much I dislike you at times. Despite that, I still love you. You are still my mother. I am not, however, going to hold my tongue in fear of what you may or may not do.
I also know that your ego will not allow you to look past your hurt to see how amazing a writer I am and share it with your friends.
You never wanted anyone to see the bad in you.

I suppose I get that from you.

With love,
Imani

SHAME, SHAME, SHAME

16 MAMA

Mama,
I hesitate to write this because I
Know what it will do to you.
When I speak, I invoke
Fear and hate in the darkest spaces within you
When, as my mother
You should love me anyway.
I took all your mean words and wore them like a
Crown around my head—allowing, walls, towers and gates to
Build up
And a moat filled with gators to be drawn.
I was the queen of my own little world.
Locked away from prying eyes so no one
Would know the dirty laundry that lie inside
We must hide.
We must hide,
So that no one knows
We must survive.
We must survive,
That's all I was told.
So, it didn't matter if it felt safe,
Because you couldn't think about
That.
All my life I struggled with
Recognizing that I was worth more
Than the moldy cheese that was
In the fridge we had to eat
Because you didn't want anyone
To take us away.
Because if you let us down you'd be alone,
And you couldn't deal with your failure.
"I gave you life," you would say
And how "thankful" I am for that.
How "thankful" I am
That my life was only worth something if
It were useful to you.
Punished like a Hebrew slave and

SHAME, SHAME, SHAME

Punished for telling the truth;
Theres so much I could say mama,
But I hesitate because I know what it will
Do to you.

17 IF I COULD SAVE HER

IF I had a choice to save her life
by giving up mine,
it would be the quickest decision
I ever made.
If I could take away
all of her pain and let her
live the life she wanted,
I would allow it in a heartbeat.
My mama bled and cried
and delt with trials I'm not even
aware of but I would give up my life
so that she could have a good one.
I'd give her a hug and kiss her once
before I said yes and bid her goodbye.
I'd thank the heavens for the chance to
hit rewind and happily watched as she lived
her life from the skies.
I wonder who my mother could have been.
I wonder what kind of person would have emerged
if she had no pain, if she got the live her life
like it should have been.
if I had a choice to save her life
by giving up mine, I'd do it in a heartbeat.
Hell, I'd do it twice.

18 OVER AND OVER AGAIN

You tried to leave me
Over and over again.
The first time I can remember
I was awoken from my sleep.
Hearing your name being screamed
Over and over again.
You said I was your reason for living.
that I kept you alive.
Over and over again.
But you tried to leave me
Every chance you got,
And I picked up the pieces.
Over and over again.
I thought it was my fault,
That very first time.
And then it happened again
And again
Over and over again.
How could my mom love me
If she didn't want to be with me?
How could she say she loved me
When she tried to leave me
Over and over again?
How could she say she loved me
When she tried to take her own life
And leave me to pick up the pieces.
Alone.
Over and over again.

SHAME, SHAME, SHAME

19 LETTER TO HURRICANE MILTON

Milton, I come before you humbly,
though not on my knees because they're
Weak.
I ask that you grant me two wishes,
One that most would not
believe.
The first I ask for grace,
To those who are trying to leave—
Slow down just a little
so there is less for us to grieve
The second I ask
And please don't judge me
For this
I ask you to take him with you.
Please carry him out to sea.
He hurt my aunts and mother and
Handled his wife so carelessly
Karma knows this man,
it already has his number
he killed children in a war
we never should have entered.
My grandfather lives in Tampa
The next city you visit on your tour.
Please grant my wishes kindly
And I'll take the punishment as a reward.
I know that asking you is nothing more
Than a coin toss—
But Milton, my family is hurting
And we will not mourn the loss.

20 FATHER

I see myself, outside myself
Reading a letter my father sent.
I hear myself, outside myself
Crying when he said he didn't want me
I feel myself, outside myself
Hoping for a father's love again
I know myself, outside myself
Willing the old hope away
Because this is a new day,
And this is a new me
A new me that doesn't wish for fatherly love
And I sometimes wonder....
Is that a good thing?

21 MISTAKE

I made a mistake when I was young
By calling my brother's father "dad"
He scrunched up his face and
Turned to me so fast, I could tell
I had made him very mad.
"I'm not your dad." He said to me
And I already knew this to be true
But he married my mom and
So he was supposed to father
Me too.
I sucked it up, but I held on to it—the
Pain he and others left.
Mistake after mistake,
I love the wrong ones and
Crumble over and over again.
I made a mistake when I was
Young and now I can't forget.
It must be perfect, or
It's all for nothing.
I'll destroy it to prove I can.

SHAME, SHAME, SHAME

22 TO BE A GIRL

I think all my life,
I've been embarrassed to be a girl.
Hear me out for a second,
my words might change your
world.
I was groomed from a young age,
So that may have obscured my view;
But to me being a girl
Was just something I couldn't do.
Girls are soft, pretty and sweet.
Girls are supposed to cry when they express their feelings.
But I was rough and played all the sports,
Ran with the boys outside in our basketball shorts.
Though as I grew older, I started to realize
The harder it was to not be a girl
In their eyes.
My lips are full and plump,
My chest too much to cover up.
My eyes did something to men,
That seemed to just pull them right in.
My mother paraded me
On the street
"Look at her
Look at she,
How old ye' think she be?"
I was 12 my dear mother,
But that was not the end for me
I learned from her then there shortly after
How *less* to be of a girl
If I *didn't* shower
I *didn't* worry
If someone would steal my **pearl**
I was teased and abused during my time in school
but dating wasn't one of my worries.
I had a crush or two, sure yeah
But I had no idea what I was doing.

SHAME, SHAME, SHAME

I learned of love from books
Where women were fighting strong.
It never occurred to me that
My view of love might have been wrong
All along.
In the real world,
you must be a girl
To be loved like a girl
And I am embarrassed of my girlhood.
How do I put down the gloves
And submit to love
If all that girlhood has hurt me?

23 MY FAULT TOO

Trigger warning: This poem was written when the author was thirteen years old and contains material related to sexual abuse against a minor child.

It was my fault too
For enjoying what he did.
It was my fault too
When I didn't tell on him.
It was my fault too
When I accepted his bribes
and played his games.
It was my fault too
For believing he wasn't the same.
It was my fault too
For not being smart enough.
It was my fault too
For getting jealous of my mother.
It was my fault too
For wishing he was mine.
It was my fault too
For letting him do it all the time.
It was my fault too
When he pulled out the whipped cream.
It was my fault too
For not running and screaming.
It was my fault too
When I asked and I begged for it.
It was my fault too
For being far too young.
It was my fault too
When I closed my mouth and pretended,
I hadn't taken part.
It was my fault too.

24 CRUSH

Trigger warning: This poem contains material related to sexual abuse against a minor child.

I had a crush on my abuser
Though I was young I felt the pull
The things he taught me
Were scary
I allowed him to stain my soul

I had a crush on my abuser
Though he wasn't mine to have
I watched him plunge himself
Into my mother
And pretended it didn't make me mad

I had a crush on my abuser
Though, many others didn't know
That I wrapped my hand around his member
Every morning
And happily watched it grow.

I had a crush on my abuser
Though I wasn't very smart
I wrote love letters to him
In school
Hidden words manifested from my heart

I had a crush on my abuser
Though, everyone thought I was reluctant
On my part
I hid behind a mask of shame
Because he said those things should only
Come out in the dark.

"Motherhood is the greatest thing and the hardest thing." ~ Ricki Lake

25 *A DEDICATION*

To my children,

You've read the worst parts of me; I'm still ashamed to have felt those things.
I hope you understand that no matter how awful I feel about myself one day, week, or month, it has nothing to do with you. You have made my world so much brighter. Most feelings are temporary, but some are forever, and the love I feel for you will never dissipate or disappear. I hope you'll be able to feel that love. I hope I can give you enough love that you never question yourselves like I questioned myself. I hope you know that no matter what the world thinks of you, you are amazing, and you deserve to love and be loved in return.

I love you,
Your mama.

SHAME, SHAME, SHAME

26 ARMS

I don't know what to say
When they trace the scars
On my arms and ask
From where they came.

I dread the day that
I must come to explain
The pain and the hurt
That caused me to self-mutilate

I don't know how they'll
React.
Will they stop seeing me as the
Superwoman who grew them
From scratch?
Will they pity me and think
The others who speak ill
On me,
Will they think their words are
Fact?

I dread the day
That they trace the scars
On my arms
And ask
"What is that?"

27 ACACIA

You started as a little bud
Nestled snugly in my womb.
The dark warmth
where you were sired,
soon then
became your tomb...
and I mourned the moment
creation had backfired.

28 I DID YOU A FAVOR

I did you a favor when
I told the women that we were with that
The holes in the walls came from me.
I did you a favor by making you something
Good to eat.
Breakfast, lunch and dinner.
I did you a favor by
giving you free use of my body
Three pregnancies and only one of them
Happy.
I did you a favor by staying so long
Because I should have left
When "Lost" became my favorite song.
I did you a favor.

29 PRO-CHOICE

This is for the moms
Who grew to love them,
Even when they didn't want to.
This is for the moms who
Dreaded every day
Closer to the date was due.
This is for the moms who
couldn't hold them
after they took their first breath,
because now yours was gone
and you struggled to catch what air was left.
This is for the moms who's hearts are so full
of love that you grew from scratch,
and this is for the moms who's hearts
opened up and you're so glad you didn't look back—
and even if you do, it's okay
to mourn the life you lost,
as long as you love the ones
you gained at the cost.
Protect and provide the
child you grew inside
and hold them dearly too,
because it was not their choice to
come here either.
Neither of you got to choose.

SHAME, SHAME, SHAME

30 HOW DO I TELL THEM

How do I tell them,
That I've finally found my peace
In the stillness of my being?
How do I tell them,
That the place I call home
Has always been with me;
In the darkest most secret place
Of my mind.
How do I tell them,
that I never would have Found it,
if I hadn't left them behind?
How do I tell them
That, although my love for them was
strong—
Strong enough to keep me living—
It didn't make me feel alive?
How do I tell them that
My heart grew three times
The days they were born,
But the weight of that love
Suffocated me.
I never even learned how to Breath on my own
And here I was teaching two others
How to master self-control.
When I had so much room left to grow.
How do I tell them
Without sounding selfish,
Without making excuses,
Or begging them to hear my case?
How do I tell them
Without revealing to them
The horrors that I escaped?
How do I tell them
That it was not their fault?
How do I tell them
When shame was all I was taught?
How do I tell them
That even though they mean
The world to me,
That the trauma I endured
Changed me.
How do you tell them
That the person who loves them the most
Loves me the least?
How do I tell them,
That person is me?

31 YOUR DADDY

Your daddy and I were in love
Once upon a time,
Even though it was a
Few months before I could
Really call Him mine.
Your mama was lonely,
Young and naïve.
She had thoughts
of ending her life.
Your daddy didn't know
How to handle someone who
Had trouble expressing their
Feelings and battled negative
Thoughts all the time.
We were angry,
and held so much in.
We were unmarried and so,
to God,
We lived in sin.
I wasn't mature enough to
Understand how things
Between us should have been.
From the beginning it was a lie,
Even though he introduced me to his kin.
he had another woman
Who lived 8 hours from we.
Whenever they fought or argued
He would take it out on me.
Twice he dragged me across the floor
To another room where I'd sleep.
The holes in the walls of your
Childhood home tells stories
Of the moments
he'll never speak.
The doors torn from their hinges
Or broken by my body flying through them.
His foot coming down on my back.
Three days later
finding out I'm pregnant.
Losing your sister
and so much more.
Your daddy's home
Was not a home to me.
To me, girls,
It was a house of horrors.
We were afraid of each other.
But somehow created such beautiful beings.
Though I regret staying with him so long
I don't regret creating you.
I **don't** regret creating you **at all**.

"Healing is a matter of time, but it is sometimes also a matter of opportunity."

~

Hippocrates

32 I TRIED

I tried smoking.
The smoke filled my lungs
And clouded my mind
Chasing the worries away
for
as long as I stayed hidden
under
Her influence.
I tried cutting because
I couldn't feel anything
And
I needed to know I was
Alive.
I needed to see
The crimson spill from
Between the lines I sliced.
I tried partying,
Ignoring the ghosts that hid
In my mental attic.
Ignoring the phone when
Those that loved me
Called in panic.
I tried to craft spells
And rhymes to manipulate
Free will and the flow of
time
And make both mine.
My favorite thing I tried,
And I'm sure others tried as
well,
I tried to bury myself in
pleasure.
Sweat dripping,
Walls echoing from moans,
But none of the vices in my
Cycle healed me when the
crisis
Came to double back at my
Door.
What can I say
Running away felt better.
It felt safer to just ignore.

33 LET GO

Everyone keeps telling me
To let go of the past
But I'm so wound up in it
That I don't know what
I'd have left.
I try, and try,
and try to move on,
But the truth is
I carry it like a debt.
I'm the garbage lady I just
A'int got paid yet--
Or pay back for all the times
I was ten toes for someone
Who only had a middle finger to give.
This is the life I
Choose.
But what am I supposed to let go
If all I've got left is garbage?

SHAME, SHAME, SHAME

34 THE COLOR OF MY SKIN

I used to hate
The color of my skin.
I didn't talk like I was black.
I didn't act like *them*.
Not one peer of mine hesitated to bring to my attention
How different I was from most of my kin.
I used to hate the tightness of my curls.
How tangled it got and how it hurt unless permed.
My little sister didn't have these problems,
Or so I wanted to believe,
My little sister is what I wanted to look like
So the outside could match who I was underneath.
I used to hate the color of my skin
But I have grown so much.
I see the beauty in my brown and have come to love my locs.
I listen to hip hop now and love
The sound because the woman I am now is a woman with soul
Who could only have grown because she had
Been buried deep, deep down.

35 THE OTHER SIDE OF PAIN

On the other side of pain is hope they say
Keep the faith and embrace the healing stage
But my heart holds many scars from the many battles
And wars that I've won.
I'm a tangled mess of broken promises and regret
With my words being my only outlet.
I'm forced into silence,
The fear of being seen gripping me
like the fingers of a child who hasn't lost
their primal instincts yet.
Razor blade nails biting into the skin around
my throat,
bleeding me of my shame.
I lean on in and pray that my journey won't
be in vain.
On the other side of pain is hope they say
But my name means faith,
It courses through my veins even though I
have no place
Hymns and chants rising from my belly
Replacing the negative energy laying stagnant
At my base. my core. my root.
Beggin me, freeing me of the past I
Want to lose.
I pray for growth and meditate on sorrow
I glue the broken pieces of my mind with
words that
Are borrowed from those who have been troubled long
Before I was sired
A tired mind yet a body that is wired.
My heart now beats way too fast
Sickness overcomes me quicker than The
Flash.
I carried it all way too long
And allowed the silence to steal my song.
If I gave up now, when I'm halfway through
I know I'd be wrong.
My whole reason for existence has been to prove
That regardless of the trials,
I'll always remain strong.
This road 'ain't for the weak and if resolution is what I truly seek then,
On the other side of pain is hope,
And that I'm gonna reach.

36 PASSING IT DOWN

I am not at fault.
Despite the shame I've carried
For the deeds done unto me
I know now, I am not at fault.
It takes breaking down completely
Leaving the shroud of their first
Impression
Abandoning the cloak of passive
Suppression
Chucking the ghost of outward
Validation
To see that I am not at fault
For the pain wrought upon me.
I did not ask him to trick me the first time
Or for love to treat me so unkind.
I did not ask to lose my sanity
Recalling all the past memories.
I did not ask to be abandoned
Over and over again when I really
Asked for love and a safe place
To rest my head.
It was not my fault, for much
Of it I was a child.
It was not my fault that I
Knew the "why" but not the "how"
On healing before I passed more pain down.

37 YUME WAS HERE

You were me when I couldn't be.
A safe and stable presence, intuitive and sweet.
You were a light when it was hard to see.
You had the freedom to write your own worlds—
Paper, pens and ink.
Sometimes I whisper to you, you let my imagination speak.
Yume was the dream, the girl I desperately wanted to be.
Yume was the author of all my greatest fantasies.
But when Yume was in danger or felt a little bit threatened,
She would run and hide from me.
Yume wasn't strong, she needed more love than me.
Yume wasn't action she was a state of being.
So, when she needed help, she'd call out to me.
She's hiding now, I can feel it,
because I have so much I need to let go.
I came back to Imani because
Imani needed to grow.
But where is Yume? Where has she gone?
I need her here so I can write my next song.
She left her mark all over my life
So that I wouldn't forget how she provided
A warm, subtle light.
So, I'm writing this now to let you know,
That Yume was here
And I won't ever let her go.

38 6 OF SWORDS

I'm not who you think I am.
I'm not who I think I am.
I am not who I was.
My independence was forced upon me,
Trust issues now keep me from
Emotionally bonding with another person
And I struggle with completing
A task unless the pressures on me.
I have to think about breathing.
It's not automatic.
It gets trapped in my chest
And even when I sing I feel the
Stinging pain under my rib where
Life used to live and every breath that
I take seems to just bypass it.
I used to have a connection to
That organ but I hung around
The wrong people
I didn't see that the food that
They gave me was poison.
I used to repeat affirmations daily
But when I met them my
Organ started failing.
My affirmations faded from my routine
And I allowed them to eat away at my self-esteem.
Little by little my organ begged
for relief
until it whittled and hid
with no strength left to live
and I forgot who I was to begin with.
I became a sponge and then a mirror,
Just begging for someone to come nearer
and pour into me so that I could see
clearer.
But no one could see the part of me that
died
And when I was forced into isolation
She had the opportunity to thrive
So I am not who you think I am.
I am not who I was.
I am not who I think I am either.
But I think this Imani,
I'm finna love.

39 LAY IT DOWN

There is a light at
The end of this tunnel
I can feel its warm rays on my
skin.
There's grace and love at my
feet,
Guiding me steadily though I
weep.
I walk and stop and gaze
At the stone and bushes that
Cross my path.
Sometimes I'm distracted, but
always
Redirected when the time has
come to
pass.
It's okay to fall.
To sit.
To rest.
This path has many trees with
canopies
To hide under when stressed.
My food only comes from the
journey and
Resting too long will only leave
me
hungry.
So I keep walking.
I keep searching.
And while I may look back a
lot,
I do,
I don't want to go back.
I breathe just as I did before
but

These butterflies that lived in
my chest
Speak to me telling me "It's
okay
To want something more.
It's okay to put down the
shame,
live your life despite the pain.
The pain only sweetens the joy
giving it a
flavor you'll never forget.
The umami of life's pleasures,
but only if
you lay it down.
The shame kept you chained
my love,
can't you see it?
The fear of being exposed has
left
You feeling lonely and
cheated.
Blaming the world.
Blaming yourself.
Missing out on your answered
cries for
help.
It's okay to lay it down now.
It's okay to live again.
It okay to love someone else
And it's okay to truly be
yourself."

40 The Cliffhanger

I was always called brave by those who knew me well.

A survivor, a leader. Someone who wouldn't let the stragglers fall behind.

"So, what are you waiting for?"

I look up at the glossy black shoes standing *just* in front of my fingertips, dangerously close to stepping on my unpainted digits. I'd have loved to pull them back but, I was stuck. If I moved even an inch, I would fall and something was keeping me from pulling myself up. A weight, heavier than a sack full of gold bars, hung on my other arm and threatened to drag me down into the dark abyss below me, as if I hadn't fought hard enough to climb my way out.

I look back up at him, eyes narrowing into a glare. "What do you mean, what am I waiting for? I need help!" I said with a bite. Couldn't he see that I was inches away from dying?

His voice came through from above me, calm, patient and resolute. "You were sent help multiple times. So. What are you waiting for?"

My eyes tried to trace the cloth of his black pants-suit legs and upward to see his face but I could only catch a glimpse of his top hat as it cast a shadow over his appearance.

"I need. Help. I can't hold on much longer and there's something trying to drag me back down!" I said between gritted teeth, the panic in my chest voicing itself as anger. It rolled and billowed up my throat like smoke as the words left my lips, threatening to choke me unless released.

The man turned slightly as he looked down and over the edge of the cliff where my legs dangled above the open chasm. He then pointed to the rope that rested just outside the reach of my right hand. I don't quite remember when it got there but it looks as though It's not even been there for as long as I have...and I've been here a while. Hanging and screaming for help.

"Your help is at the other end of that rope there. You just need to take it." His finger followed the rope up and past him where a crowd of people stood, smiling and waving with their collective expressions of support as they held firmly to the other end of the rope.

I turned back to him, just as angry as before only now--heat began to rise up my neck. "I don't know them! What if they cut the rope before I'm safe?! What if they gossip about how I was too weak to pull myself up?!"

The man turned toward me again, hat tilting forward as if trying to look closer at me. "Why would they do that?" He asked. He sounded genuinely confused, his deep and bodiless voice echoing around me; the eeriness of It bouncing off the rocks of the cliff I clung to.

"Because it happened before, why wouldn't they?!" I said instinctively.

He sighed loudly, as if we had had this conversation many times before but I don't remember meeting him a day in my life. He was a stranger just as they were. He couldn't tell me what to do or get upset because I didn't want to do what HE wanted me to do!

"Child, listen to yourself. Does this even make sense? You ask for help and then deny yourself the chance for assistance before you can experience it."

"--Because I already KNOW they'll let go! If my own family would leave me, then why wouldn't they?!" I turn a pointed look to the broken rope on the other side of my arm, its frayed edges gently blowing in the wind looking despondent at this altitude. "Look! If my own family would let me go, then why wouldn't they? My family left me here, hanging as if I was nothing!"

He was quiet for a moment, as if he was studying me. "And who would you like to help you?" He asked slowly.

I averted my gaze, guilt and shame pulling tears to the corners of my eyes. I said nothing. I can't trust my voice.

His voice grew softer when he spoke next. Softer, but deeper as if he needed to make sure I heard him to my core, as if this was the final time he would dare to interject. "If you're still holding that rope, a rope that is broken, frayed and detached... then I assume you're hoping they'll come back and try to fix it. I assume you want them to see that you still hold hope for them and that they will help you fix what they broke. Is that correct?"

The tears poured out from behind my glare before I could stop them. "Yes. I'm still holding on but no one has even looked back...they don't even stand by the rope anymore. Not just my family... friends... lovers... they all were just okay that I left...that they left me..."

The man in the top hat knelt down in front of me then, his hands gloved in black leather. He picked up the new rope, the one with people waiting, and held it out to me. "So, what are you waiting for? Let go and grab on."

What did he mean? My other hand was still weighed down, restricting me from reaching for the rope. If I let go, I'd fall. "I can't! I don't have the space! There's something stopping me!"

"Let. Go."

I looked away and down at the hand being restrained only...it wasn't restrained. I was still holding the other end of the frayed rope. I was still holding on to the pain my family left me. I was still holding onto the shame they gave me. I was still holding on to the time that I lost. I was still holding onto the high price of cost. I'm still holding onto the image they created for me but to save myself I can't take them with me. I have to let them go.

So, I let go of the fray and grab onto the whole. The rope connected to people who will struggle to let me go. And when I turn to thank the man, he was gone as if he had already known.

ABOUT THE AUTHOR

Miss Imani is a Maryland-born Black American woman who started reading and writing at only four years old. She adopted a love for reading later in her childhood and soon became engrossed in her own world, where she controlled the story. Miss Imani started publishing her short stories, poems, and poetic art on sites such as DeviantArt under the username raven202. She later started writing fanfiction on Fanfiction.net under the username Theutsukushiiyume, where she currently has multiple stories with large followings. Miss. Imani took time away from writing to deal with her personal life and is now back to writing under her real name, sharing her poetry (and life) with the world.

About The Illustrator

Pamela Walsh is a multifaceted artist and poet. She uses acrylics, watercolors, graphite and ink to illustrate stories. Her eclectic style creates a unique body of work across many media and art genres. Her philosophy is to let her art and poetry become what it needs to be for her own healing journey, as well as to challenge others' assumptions and thought habits. She can most easily be found on tiktok as PamelaWalshArts, and contacted for commissions at PamelaWalshArts@yahoo.com

www.ingramcontent.com/pod-product-compliance
Lightning Source LLC
Chambersburg PA
CBHW071231160426
43196CB00012B/2475